cuba
land of spirit

"Music and rhythm find their way into the secret places of the soul."

Plato

"Rhythm is something you either have or don't have, but when you have it, you have it all over."

Elvis Presley

cuba
land of spirit

Photographs by **James Sparshatt**

Havana Club

El Ron de Cuba

Cuba *Land of Spirit*
Photographs by James Sparshatt

First Edition

Published in the United Kingdom in 2006 by BedBury Press,
3 Bedfordbury, London WC2N, UK.

www.capitalculture.eu

ISBN 0-9553709-0-6 | 978-0-9553709-0-8

British Library Cataloguing-in-Publication Data.
A catalogue record for this book is available from the British Library.

Printed and bound in Verona, Italy by Editoriale Bortolazzi-Stei.

CONTENTS

CUBA   *Land of Spirit*

I spent the latter half of the nineties in the Andes, working as a mountain guide in Peru and a photojournalist in Bolivia. It was a fascinating experience that allowed me to learn much about local culture, but never really to transcend the role of mere observer. The Andean world is dominated by natural forces, by the Gods of the earth, the sun and the rain and the spirits of the mountains. The people are mysterious, you scratch at the surface of understanding, slowly breaching the barriers of ingrained suspicion, but true insight remains elusive.

My first impressions of Cuba in 1999 were quite the opposite of this closed world. It appeared to offer itself up to the visitor. Doors were readily thrown open, friends easily made.

My camera gave me an excuse to delve a little deeper. A reason to search out a beautiful dancer, to sit and share a bottle of rum with a musician, to indulge my pleasures… to dance and to entertain. I found myself hanging around street corners, watching moments of emotional intensity, love and laughter unfold.

The photographic opportunities were endless. Amidst the dilapidated buildings life was being lived to the full, immersed in a music that appeared to emerge from every doorway, a surreal moment seemingly around each corner. A frail 80-year-old man would be flirting outrageously with a young woman, her lycra bodice stretched to bursting point; a group of school children would begin to dance with a rhythm and confidence beyond their years. It was captivating.

There was no change in behaviour when my camera came out. The Cubans neither shied away, nor played-up, to its enquiring lens. They just remained who they were, take me or leave me and the devil may care…

Their attitude transcended the challenges of life, and was at once both charming and beguiling. Under a Caribbean sun, with rum and music in abundance, a complex union, part Spanish *duende*, part African *orisha*, has produced a wonderful hybrid.

This book is a personal celebration of their enthralling spirit.

JAMES SPARSHATT

CUBANÍA

My work with Havana Club International regularly leads to conversations about the phenomenon that is Cuba. One aspect of our lives in particular dominates these discussions, something we like to call *Cubanía*.

The concept of *Cubanía* has as many nuances as there are people, nevertheless optimism and positive thinking, the ability to laugh even in the worst of times, and the pride we take in being Cuban are aspects that are ever present.

This Cuban spirit is the result of the mixture of the Spanish, the African and a hint of the Chinese. A melting pot that has defined our history, our approach to life and our lifestyles. It has grown with our culture and been refined throughout the development of our nation.

Havana Club, our rum, is also part of this history and as with our people it is the quality of the blend that makes us unique and ultimately Cuban.

This collection of photographs will give you a much closer understanding of our *Cubanía*.

SERGIO VALDES DORTA
Export Director
Havana Club International S.A.

Chapter 1

Harmony of Spirit

The rhythm and spirit of Cuba evolved from two distinct cultures that share a common exuberance for life. From Spain came a love of romance and dance, from Africa a raw and passionate soul. This melting pot produced a new and vibrant society; one of natural ebullience... with a fire in its belly and a coquettish smile on its lips.

"Cuba is a cocktail, its spirit is mestizo. And it is from this spirit that a definitive colour will come to our skin. Some day they will say Cuban colour!"

Nicolás Guillén

Armonía

A duality of male and female, black and white... each a subconscious but integral part of the other.

From ivory to darkest mahogany...
and every shade in between.

The streets of Havana are never quiet.
Music and the sounds of laughter are
almost a constant companion, a sort of
soundtrack to life... girls strut to a rhythm
and dominoes are smashed down to a beat...

14

Battered and bruised by the Atlantic storms that periodically ravage Havana, el Malecón is a place of meeting, of strolling troubadours and of romantic interlude...

A wave smashes against the sea wall and the girls are enveloped in a plume of water. It soaks their uniforms, but can't dampen their enthusiasm for life...

La Sonrisa

Each Sunday the group of friends gather on Havana's sea wall. They swim and dance and laugh.
Her smile is of joy, a perfect picture of happiness...

La Dama

The Cuban spirit shines brightly even from behind a cloud of cigar smoke. Her eyes reveal the depth of pride within...

Puro... Alegría

She sits on her step just off Plaza Catedral, posing for the tourists at a dollar a go. Her cigar remains firmly clamped between her teeth, her view of the world shrouded in smoke...

Chapter 2

A Heritage of Spanish Romance

Cuba was a Spanish colony for over 400 years. Settlers came from Galicia and Catalonia, Andalucia and the Canaries. They brought with them a love of romance and sensuality expressed in the literature of Cervantes and musical traditions from the fandango to the flamenco. They danced to the strum of the guitar, dresses swirling, clapping and beating their heels to the rhythms of their homeland...

"Lean your body forward slightly to support the guitar against your chest, for the poetry of the music should resound in your heart."

Andrés Segovia

Esperanza

It is late afternoon and after five days of music,
drinking and dancing till dawn the world is a
little scratchy. Monica begins to tune Dagoberto's aged
guitar, the dusk light illuminates her face and reflects
in her eyes...

Dagoberto

He has been playing music in the Casa de la Trova of
Holguin for 50 years. His body is now bent and his
fingers are gnarled, but still he carries his guitar
and is always ready to sing or reminisce over a glass
of rum...

The first rays of sun warm the air and still nobody is ready to go to bed. The guitar has been passed back and forth all night. Each trova singer trying to outdo the last in the wit and insight of their poetry put to music. It's a tradition that stretches back to the 19th century... of troubadours and their stories of life's problems and love's glories...

"Trova sin trago se traba"
Trova chokes without a drink
Anon

She sings as if her heart will burst, a bolero of love...
eternal but unrequited...

The words of Dos Gardenias float in the air, talking of love and two hearts entwined, as couples dance tight in each other's arms...

"My soul tremulous and lonely
At nightfall will grow forlorn.
There's a show, let us go see
The Spanish dancer perform."

José Martí

"The great artists of the south of Spain, whether they sing, dance or play, know that no emotion is possible without the arrival of the Duende (spirit)."

Federico García Lorca

Orgullo
...from the impossible dreams of youth, through
the confidence of sexual maturity to the power
behind the scenes...

Chapter 3

An Undercurrent of African Passion

The passion of Africa beats strong in the heart of Cuba. It arrived with the elemental, pulsating rhythms of a myriad tribal groups and traditions. It survived through the cults that refused to forget their ancient Gods even as they were subsumed into a syncretic version of Christianity. It flourished, again, as the drums of the past were reborn as the driving rhythmic force of the island's music.

*"our song
our simple song
is like a muscle under
the skin of the soul"*

Nicolás Guillén

The beat of the tumbadora is relentless as the drummer summons Changó, the God of thunder, passion and virility... around his neck hang the coloured beads of a believer as rivulets of sweat run down his body.

It is her Saint's day and an altar of offerings is set up for Ochún, Goddess of love, money and happiness. She's already spent a year dressed in white, abstaining from alcohol, sugar and sex and now she's an accepted member of the religion of Santeria... soon the drums will start and the celebration begin...

Callejón de Hammel is an alleyway hidden away in the heart of Vedado. For six days of the week it is quiet, only the murals and graffiti attesting to another life. On Sunday it awakens to the sound of rumba, the music of slavery; a lament to the suffering and an incantation to the ancient spirits... the singing is harsh, the beat driving, the atmosphere steamy.

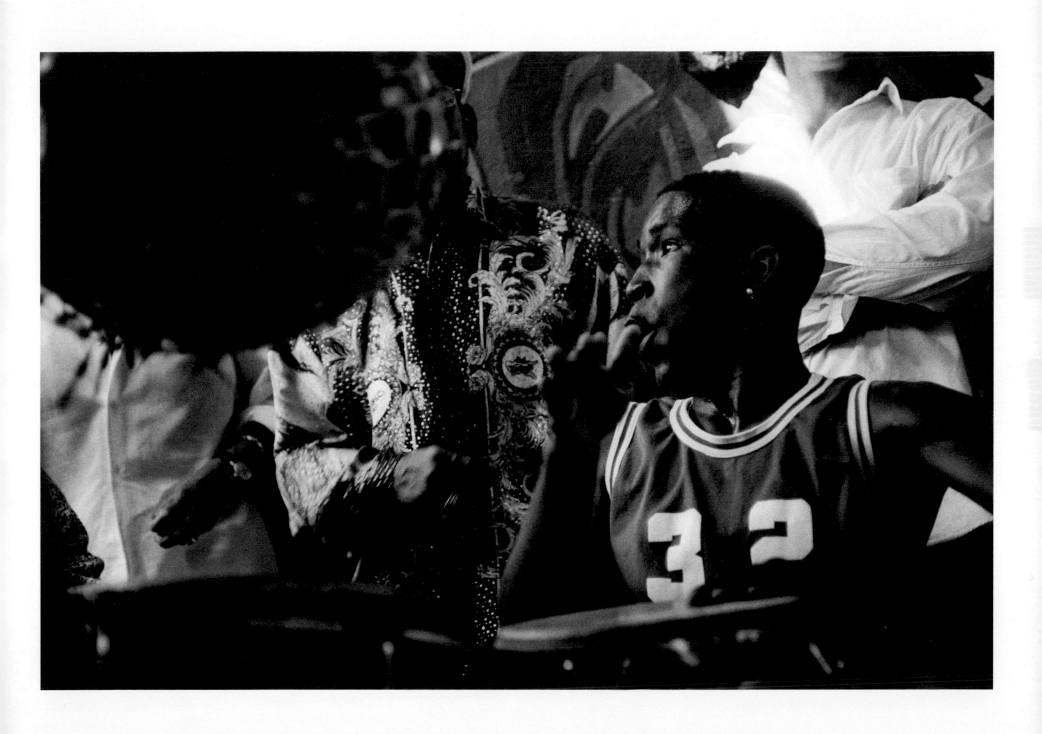

La Telaraña (the spider's web)
The men dance to conquer their partners.
They tease and strut even as the women
feign disinterest. Slowly they are drawn
into a web, until they are trapped in its
dangerous heart...

Club Tropicana

*The dancers swagger across the stage bedecked in
feathers and sequins, dripping sensuality and sweat.
The colours of their costumes and the rhythms of the
dance tell of African dreams and passions...*

Chapter 4

Rhythms of Emotion

*From these two diverse roots a new music evolved.
The guitar in harmony with the drum, romance
imbued with passion under the Caribbean sun.
Spain and Africa gave birth to a people with a voice
of their own and they called this voice Son...*

*"Let the heartwarming Son break out
And our people dance
Heart close to heart
Glasses clinking together
Water on water with rum"*

Nicolás Guillén

Havana Café

Calle Obispo runs through the heart of Old Havana. It's a street of bars soaked in the rhythm of Son. El Escabeche is about halfway along, a tiny place barely big enough for a band. Markia is singing in front of an audience for the first time, the nerves are gone, the music has taken control...

"In Cuba music is... like eating,
breathing and sleeping.
It is an integral part of living."

Wim Wenders

It is almost 3am when Marcia's all-girl teenage band begins to play. They have waited three days for the opportunity, and now they are ready to impress the audience of more established musicians gathered on the roof of the museum. Then it starts to rain. A room is rapidly cleared and the band is moved indoors and soon the rhythms of Son sweep everyone to their feet. Instruments are swapped back and forth, everybody wants their turn to play and nobody leaves before dawn.

"On with the dance!
Let joy be unconfined;
No sleep till morn, when Youth and Pleasure meet
To chase the glowing hours with flying feet."

Lord Byron

Chapter 5

A Celebration of Life

Cubans have an innate ability to enjoy whatever opportunities life throws at them. Smiles are free, music is everywhere, to dance is to give expression to life, to flirt is to give it meaning. It is an attitude that infects all but the coldest of hearts, a belief in celebrating life and sharing love...

*"Ya llegó
la felicidad"*
*happiness
has arrived*

Pupy Pedroso

*"Joy is not in things,
it is in us"*

Richard Wagner

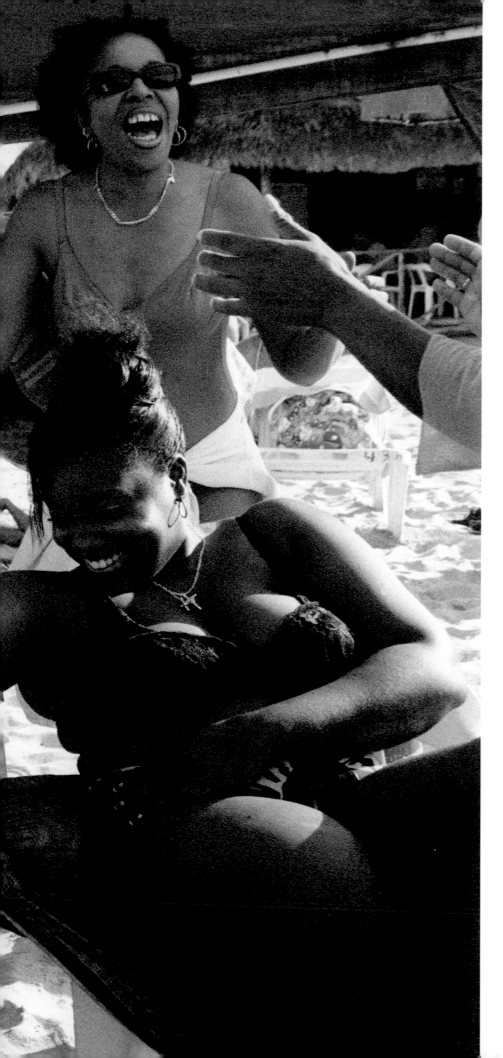

Playa Santa María

The girls of Rumba Morena scramble off the bus and head for the ocean, carrying their tumbodoras, their claves and their cowbells. As the sun begins to dip they set up on the sand, their laughter filling the air. They start to play and the whole beach gathers round...

Casa de las Tradiciones

*It is a warm sultry Santiago evening. The backyard
of the old Casa de las Tradiciones is filled with
friends. They have sung together for many years,
each has a beautiful voice, each a song to sing...*

May 1st

The crowds gather in Revolutionary Square to celebrate workers' day. There are perhaps a quarter of a million people standing shoulder to shoulder... as they leave the drums begin, and the dancing... a conga that lasts for hours as they slowly return to their barrios.

An Exuberant Soul

No excuse is needed, no location sought... an instrument and a few friends is all that is required...

A New Generation

The school kids are walking to their next class when they hear the music. It wafts along the street and soon they find its rhythm. They begin to dance and the energy and enthusiasm of youth takes hold.

"I am certain that after the dust of centuries has passed over our cities, we, too, will be remembered not for victories or defeats in battle or in politics, but for our contribution to the human spirit."

John Fitzgerald Kennedy

NOTES ON THE PHOTOGRAPHS

COVER
Havana Café, Markia singing in el Escabeche,
Havana 2002

2   *El Deseo*, girl in Casa de la Trova, Trinidad 1999
El Viaje, on the tour bus leaving Las Romerías de Mayo,
Holguín 2000
5   Man from Centro Havana 2002

HARMONY OF SPIRIT
9   *Armonía*, school of dance, Santa Clara, 2001
10   Farmer, Manicaragua 2006
Girl, Centro Havana 2003
Woman, Havana Vieja 2002
Dancer, Santiago de Cuba 2006
Girl, calle Obispo, Havana Vieja 2005
11   Girl, Centro Havana 2005
Woman, Santiago de Cuba 2006
Percussionist, Havana Vieja 2003
Babalawo (santería priest), Centro Havana 2004
El Dandy, calle Obispo, Havana Vieja 2004

Streets of Life
12   The Cuban strut… calle Obispo, Havana Vieja 2001
13   Playing *dominó*, Centro Havana 2005
14   *El Vaquero Perdido*, the cowboys of Cuba sit bolt
upright in their saddles and exude pride, calle Obispo,
Havana Vieja 2003
15   A character of calle Obispo, Havana Vieja 2002
16   Dressed up for a party, Centro Havana 2005
17   Ron Cubano, Centro Havana 2005

El Malecón
18   The Atlantic swell sends waves crashing over the
sea wall, Havana 2000
20   Friends and lovers relax on the sea wall, Havana 2001
21   Young love on el Malecón, Havana 2003
22   Schoolgirls celebrating on May 1st are soaked by a
sudden wave, Havana 2003
24   The Florida coast is only 90 miles from
El Malecón, Havana 2002
25   *La Sonrisa*, the perfect smile, Havana 2002

The Cuban Spirit
26   *La Dama del Callejón*, Centro Havana 2005
28   81-year-old Graciela, Havana Vieja 2005
29   Girl in Hanabanilla, Villa Clara 2005
30   Mother and daughter, Havana Vieja 2006
Brother and sister, Centro Havana 2002
31   Mother and daughter, Jibacoa 2002
32   Artist's model, Holguín 2003
33   *Puro… Alegría*, Havana Vieja 2001

A HERITAGE OF SPANISH ROMANCE
35   *Las Curvas*, a girl and her guitar in harmony,
Holguín 2002

The Spanish Guitar
36   *Esperanza*, late afternoon at Las Romerías de Mayo,
Holguín 2002
37   *Dagoberto*, celebrating in the Casa de la Trova,
Holguín 2002
38   Ernesto Rodriguez of Postrova and Diego Cano,
Holguín 2000
Rolando Berrio, Santa Clara 2005
39   Practice in the Casa de la Cultura, Santiago de Cuba 2006
40   *La Soledad*, Israel of Buena Fé, Casa de la Trova,
Holguín 2000
41   Victor Quiñones, Las Romerías de Mayo, Holguín 2003

Los Boleros
42   Bolero in the Museum of Rum, Havana Vieja 2002
43   At the piano, Palacio de Valle, Cienfuegos 2006
44   Las Divas, Santiago de Cuba 2001
45   Singing a bolero with Pachi playing in the
background, Holguín 2000

Spanish Dance
46   Fandango in front of the Capitolio, Centro Havana 2000
47   School of Spanish Dance, Gran Teatro, Havana 2002

48   *La Practica*, Gran Teatro, Havana 2002
49   *La Concentración*, Gran Teatro, Havana 2002
50   Flamenco, Holguín 2003
51   School of Spanish Dance, Gran Teatro, Havana 2003
52   *La Escuela*, Gran Teatro, Havana 2003
53   *Reflexiones*, Gran Teatro, Havana 2002
54   *Orgullo*, Festival Iboamericano, Holguín 2000
55   *Las Manos*, Holguín 2003

AN UNDERCURRENT OF AFRICAN PASSION
57   *El Amor*, Plaza Catedral, Havana Vieja 2002

The African Drum
58   *Rumba de Cuba*, loading the drums en route to the Weimilere
Festival, Centro Havana 2004
59   Playing *las tumbadoras*, Santiago de Cuba 2006
60   Playing a double headed *batá* drum of the
Lucumí Yoruba, Santiago de Cuba 2006
61   Rumba Morena on the bus to the beach,
Ciudad del Este 2006
Rumba Morena playing in Callejón de Hammel,
Vedado 2004
62   Sunday rumba in barrio Tivoli, Santiago de Cuba 2006
63   Sunday rumba in barrio Tivoli, Santiago de Cuba 2006

Santería
64   Offerings to the *orishas* on a saint's day,
Centro Havana 2006
66   Dressing as *Ochún*, Goddess of Love, Centro Havana 2006
67   Folkloric dancers, Weimilere Festival, Guanabacoa 2004
68   Celebration of the *orishas* at home, Centro Havana 2006
69   A saint's day, Señor Ofarrill with his "percussionist's"
wheel chair, Centro Havana 2006
70   Afro-Cuban folklore, Plaza de Armas, Havana Vieja 2004
71   Irosa Obba at the Weimilere Festival, Guanabacoa 2004

Rumba in el Callejón
72   The *Coro* (chorus) of Irosa Obba, Callejón de Hammel 2005
73   Drummer, Callejón de Hammel 2006
74   Dancing the Guaguancó, Callejón de Hammel 2005
75   Drummer, Callejón de Hammel 2006
76   Dancing, Callejón de Hammel 2005
77   Leonel playing the *guagua*, a split length of bamboo,
Callejón de Hammel 2004

Afro-Cuban Dance
78   *La Telaraña*, a school of dance in a roofless building
that doubles as a hard rock nightclub. The students are
practicing Afro-Cuban folkloric dances, Santa Clara 2001
80   School of dance, Santa Clara 2001
81   School of dance, Santa Clara 2001
82   Rehearsals at Club Tropicana, Havana 2002
83   Rumba group rehearsing dance moves, Santiago de
Cuba 2006
84   A break in rehearsals under the watchful eyes of Ché and
Fidel, Santiago de Cuba 2006
85   Folkloric dancers in rehearsal, Las Romerías de Mayo,
Holguín 2003

Club Tropicana
86   A dancer performs in Club Tropicana, Miramar 2005
87   A dancer from Club Tropicana in Plaza Catedral,
Havana Vieja 2002
88   Dancers in Club Tropicana, Miramar 2005
Dancer in Club Tropicana, Miramar 2005
89   *La Reina del Hielo*, a dancer in Club Tropicana,
Miramar 2005

RHYTHMS OF EMOTION
91   *Havana Café*, Markia performing in bar El Escabeche,
calle Obispo, Havana Vieja 2001

Son de la Calle
92   Las Perlas del Son, Santiago de Cuba 2006
93   Son Caliente, Casa de la Musica, Santiago de Cuba 2006
94   Singer, Café Paris 2000
96   *La Risa*, Café Paris 1999
97   Markia playing the clave, bar El Bosque, calle Obispo,
Havana 2006

98   Son being enjoyed in Plaza Catedral, Havana Vieja 2001
99   The audience responds to Sonrisa Caribeña, bar
El Escabeche, calle Obispo, Havana 2006

Las Romerías de Mayo
100   Jacquelin de Las Perlas del Son singing after a cancelled
concert, Las Romerías de Mayo, Holguín 2000
101   Singing *controversias*, a musical battle of invention,
Las Romerías de Mayo, Holguín 2000
An impromptu concert after the rain, Las Romerías de Mayo,
Holguín 2000
102   *Trovadores* singing in the rehearsal room, Las Romerías
de Mayo, Holguín 2000

A Love of Dance
103   Salsa dancing, Baracoa 2001
104   Dancing salsa at Las Romerías de Mayo, Holguín 2003
105   Dancing salsa at Las Romerías de Mayo, Holguín 2000
106   Dancing at Las Romerías de Mayo, Holguín 2003
Dancing at Las Romerías de Mayo, Holguín 2003
107   Dancing at home at 4am, Holguín 2003

A CELEBRATION OF LIFE
109   Celebración, she gifted me her smile and was gone into the
darkness… Festival Iboamericano, Holguín 2000
110   Beatriz, Centro Havana 2005
111   Backstage at a Candido Fabre concert, Media Luna 2006
Singer from Los Mambisas, Havana Vieja 2002

Playa Santa María
112   Rumba Morena, Christmas Day, Playa Santa María 2004
114   Rumba Morena, Christmas Eve, Playa Santa María 2005
115   Maningo and friend, Christmas Eve, Playa Santa María 2005
Rumba Morena, Christmas Day, Playa Santa María 2004
116   Dancing, Playa Santa María 2001
117   Musician with his double bass, Playa Santa María 2001

Casa de las Tradiciones
118   Singers in Casa de las Tradiciones, Santiago de Cuba 2001
120   Chinese cornet, Casa de las Tradiciones, Santiago de Cuba 2001
121   Singing a bolero in Casa de las Tradiciones, Santiago de Cuba 2001
Singing a bolero in Casa de las Tradiciones, Santiago de Cuba 2001
Musicians in Casa de las Tradiciones, Santiago de Cuba 2001

May 1st
122   May Day celebrations, Plaza Revolución, Havana 2003
124   An image of Che Guevara, May 1st, Plaza Revolución, Havana 2001
125   A group of school teachers, May 1st, Havana 2002
Dancing conga in the barrio after May 1st celebrations,
Centro Havana 2003
126   Army cadets dancing in the conga, May 1st, Havana 2001
Army cadets waiting to march past Fidel Castro, May 1st,
Havana 2001
127   Army cadets at May Day celebrations, Plaza Revolución,
Havana 2001

An Exuberant Soul
128   Friends, Havana Vieja 2004
129   Bus ride, Havana 2004
130   An afternoon in the Casa de la Trova, Holguín 2003
Enjoying the music in the Casa de la Trova, Holguín 2003
131   Workers from a local pharmacy celebrate a birthday, Havana 2006
132   Dancing to NG la Banda, Festival Iboamericano, Holguín 2000
133   Dance practice, Santiago de Cuba 2006

A New Generation
134   School kids dancing on calle Obispo, Havana 2001
136   Boys, Santiago de Cuba 2001
137   After the rainstorm, Havana 2002
138   The ballet school at the opening procession of Las Romerías
de Mayo, Holguín 2001
139   Students dancing in the opening procession of Las Romerías
de Mayo, Holguín 2003
140   On top of the Loma de la Cruz (hill of the cross), at the start
of Las Romerías de Mayo, Holguín 2003

Back Cover
Candita Batista still singing at 89, Casa de la Trova,
Camaguey 2006
Ruicho with his music collection, Guanabacoa 2004

QUOTED WRITERS

Plato (c427-c347BC)
Plato believed the arts had a powerful effect both on behaviour and character. In his philosophy on the ideal republic he insisted that music (especially music), along with poetry, drama and the other arts, should be an integral part of the educational development of young citizens.

Nicolás Guillén (1902-1989)
Guillén was born in the Cuban town of Camaguey in 1902, just 20 years after the formal end of slavery. His parents were both of mixed African and Spanish stock and he was often subjected to racism and discrimination. His poetry thus carried an edge of social activism, conditioned by experience. In 1930, he published *Motivos de Son*, probably his seminal work. The eight poems describe the daily living conditions of Cuban blacks in their own Afro-Cuban vernacular, using many words that imitate the sound of drums or the rhythm of son. Guillén was eventually to become Cuba's poet laureate; his work has inspired generations of Cuban musicians, artists and poets. These translations were published in "*The Poetry of Nicolás Guillén*" by Dennis Sardinha (1976), and have been reproduced by kind permission of New Beacon Books Ltd.

José Martí (1853-1895)
Jose Martí is Cuba's national hero, the father of their independence. He is considered one of the Hispanic world's leading writers and thinkers - a man whose views on equality and social justice had a huge influence on the 20th century. As a young idealist his criticisms of Spanish colonial rule and his demands for Cuban self-determination resulted in exile. Over the next 20 years he lived in Spain, Mexico, Venezuela and the US, constantly expounding on, and planning, a Cuban revolt that would lead the country to an independence free of foreign interference. In 1895 he was killed in one of the first skirmishes of that revolt. The verse is from the poem "*The Spanish Dancer*".

Andrés Segovia (1893-1987)
Segovia was instrumental in founding the modern classical guitar movement. His technical brilliance and artistry did much to raise the instrument's profile at a time when it was considered suitable only for bars and celebrations. His legacy is the acceptance of the guitar on the concert stage.

Federico García Lorca (1898-1936)
García Lorca was born in Granada, Spain and became a poet and playwright of great power. He was a contemporary of Picasso and a friend of Luis Buñuel and Salvador Dalí. His work often reflects on the troubled side of humanity with a great emphasis on the influence of death on the living. He was fascinated by the flamenco of his homeland and the passion and angst of its themes. In 1933 he gave a lecture in Havana entitled "*Play and Theory of the Duende (spirit)*", expounding his theory that great art depends upon a vivid awareness of death, a connection with a nation's soil, and an acknowledgment of the limitations of reason. In 1936 he was captured by Falangist soldiers during the Spanish Civil War, dragged into a field, shot and buried in an unmarked grave.

Wim Wenders (1945-)
Wenders is an award-winning German film director who has worked both in Europe and America. His credits include *Paris, Texas* and *Buena Vista Social Club*. The latter documentary brought the golden greats of Cuban music to world attention and did much to revitalize interest in the island and its people.

Lord George Gordon Byron (1788-1824)
One of England's most famous poets and romantic figures. An adventurer and womaniser who scandalized the British establishment but whose exploits and passion for life became legendary. His attitudes, as expressed through his often autobiographical poetry, would have made him ideally suited to a life in Cuba! The verse is an extract from *Childe Harold's Pilgrimage*.

Pupy Pedroso (1946-)
César "Pupy" Pedroso is one of the key figures in the last three decades of Cuban popular music. A pianist and prolific composer, he gained fame while playing with Orquesta Revé and then as a founding member of Los Van Van, perhaps Cuba's most famous dance band. In 2001, he left to form his own group, "Pupy y Los Que Son Son". The lyric is from the song "*Te molesta que sea feliz*".

John F Kennedy (1917-1963)
JFK is inextricably linked to Cuba through his involvement in the Bay of Pigs and the Cuban Missile crisis. His words however have a universal resonance that cut across cultural boundaries and national borders. Cuba is a place that lives through its music and the spirit of its people, this is truly their gift to the world.

All other text James Sparshatt.

TERMS

Dominoes
Dominoes (*Dominó*) is a national game in Cuba. For many players it is a daily social event. Games are very competitive with a lot of shouting and slamming down of tiles (*fichas*). The Cuban version is played in pairs, with partners priding themselves on their mutual understanding and use of complex strategies. The fichas have from 0 to 9 dots and a team wins a round when all ten of one player's tiles have been placed.

El Malecón
Havana's sea promenade, el Malecón, stretches 7km from Old Havana to the embassy district. Its construction began in 1901 and continued for 20 years. It's now a place where people go to meet, drink and carouse, where kids throw themselves into the Atlantic swell, fishermen float in inner tubes and offerings are given to Yemaya, Santería Goddess of the Sea.

Trova
Trova, the music of the trovadores, or troubadours, began life in the country around Santiago in the east of Cuba. It was the music of the itinerant showman, simple ballads sung to the accompaniment of the guitar. In the early 20th century it arrived in Havana and rapidly became a popular form of musical expression. After the Revolution artists such as Pablo Milanes and Silvio Rodriguez created Nueva Trova as a vehicle for social commentary.

Casa de la Trova
Most cities in Cuba gained a Casa de la Trova in the 60s or 70s. Old colonial houses were converted into venues for musicians to play son and trova or sing boleros. They became the central point of community life where musical traditions could be preserved, and octogenarians could play alongside a new generation of artists.

Bolero
The Cuban bolero is sultry and romantic, largely influenced by European song but with a hint of African percussion to give it spice. It too originated in the east of Cuba before migrating to Havana and going on to touch the hearts of the world.

El Duende
The Spanish consider the *duende* to be something akin to the spirit of the earth. A force that we are all capable of feeling, but which none of us can explain. When the flamenco is danced or played the *duende* must be summoned to take control; without the *duende*, it is said, there can be no passion just a cheap pretence.

La Tumbadora
The Tumbadora, often known as the conga, is based on the ancestral *batá* drums of West Africa.

Callejón de Hammel
The alleyway of Hammel in Vedado is named after a French-German gun-runner who lived there during the 19th century. In 1990 it was transformed by the work of Cuban sculptor and painter Salvador Gonzáles. His murals and other pieces of art produced by local residents became a focal point for black Afro-Cuban culture. The space is now used for workshops and community self-improvement programs. Every Sunday it comes alive as bands play rumba to celebrate the *orishas*, ancient spirits of Africa.

Santería
Santería is the main African-derived religion of Cuba. Most of its beliefs can be traced to the Lucumí Yoruba culture of northern Nigeria, though words and Gods from other regions have also been incorporated. The religion has a single supreme God, *Olodumare*, and a pantheon of guardian spirits, or *orishas*, that influence all aspects of life. Each *orisha* has a Catholic saint or virgin counterpart, a sacred set of colours and a distinctive rhythm on the drums.

Changó
The God of fire, lightning and dance. His sacred colours are red and white. He is the owner of the *batá*, the double-headed drums of the Lucumí Yoruba.

Ochún
The Goddess of love, beauty, money and happiness. She is represented by Our Lady of Charity (*La Virgen de la Caridad del Cobre*), Cuba's patron saint. Her colours are gold, bright yellow and orange.

Rumba
Rumba is the drum-based music that provides a direct link to the island's African heritage. Three drummers (the *obatala*) and a series of cowbells and claves provide the percussive rhythm, while a lead singer and chorus sing incantations to the Gods. The most common form of Cuban rumba is the *Guaguancó* in which a man and woman dance. The male symbolically attempts to make sexual contact with his partner via a thrown arm or pelvic thrust, called suggestively the *vacunao* or vaccination. She entices him closer and then defends herself with a turn or a protective hand.

Son
Son grew out of the country music of eastern Cuba. It combined Spanish string instruments with African drums, introduced Cuban inventions such as the percussive clave, and developed a vocal style that encouraged listeners to dance. Son greats such as Miguel Matamoros and later Beny Moré were hugely influential in the development of a Latin American music movement that has brought the son derivative, salsa, to a massive world audience.

Las Romerías de Mayo
Holguín is a provincial capital in the east of the island. In the early nineties a tradition of harvest festivals was revitalised as a celebration of music and dance. The event is supported by Hermanos Saiz, Cuba's youth culture and arts organisation, which brings trova players, Afro-Cuban folklore groups, Cuban hip-hop bands, poets and painters together for a week-long celebration.

Playa Santa María
The beach of Santa María is forty minutes by car from downtown Havana. A place to swim in the deep blue of the Atlantic, listen to a Cuban rhythm, drink a mojito and soak up the Caribbean sun.

ACKNOWLEDGEMENTS

I arrived in Havana for the first time in 1999 to find my supposed accommodation full. It was late; I was disoriented and had nowhere to stay. The doorman of the hotel took me to a rather cramped *casa particular* on a noisy *avenida*. The night was steamy and my hosts were barely audible over the pumping stereo. A Tuesday at 2am seems a strange time to start a party, but my arrival ensured that there were funds to buy a couple of bottles of Havana Club rum and no more excuse was needed. The neighbours were invited in, the stereo raised a notch and we danced all night. Welcome to Cuba!

On my many return visits to the island Havana Club became one of my closest companions. A *mojito* was often the icebreaker in friendships that lasted a few hours or many years. In London, some years later, I approached the brand's marketing manager, Crispin Stephens, to sponsor my first exhibition. Havana Club have been supportive of my work ever since. This has included exhibitions at the World Music Festival in Glasgow, the Black Film Awards in London and three months at the National Theatre.

Their support grew considerably when John Lynch took the marketing lead. His immediate enthusiasm when the idea of the book was first postulated did much to encourage me to continue and bring the work to fruition. The cover photograph, Havana Café, was used for their first nationwide advertising campaign, and a number of the images in this book are used to enhance the atmosphere of their Piece of Havana events held across the UK.

On that first trip I was shown around Cuba by Ernesto Noriega. He introduced me to many aspects of his island home and has helped me on my every visit since. He opened my eyes to his country through his kindness and generosity and I am deeply grateful.

My true conversion, however, came a year later when I stumbled on to Las Romerías de Mayo festival in the city of Holguín. The festival celebrates the diversity of Cuban music and youth culture and includes Afro-Cuban rumba, son, salsa, new trova and even Cuban hip hop and thrash rock. I spent long afternoons listening to trova singers while bottles of rum were passed from hand to hand; watched couples dancing salsa on the roof of La Caligari under a starlit sky and revelled in the chance to meet so many musicians, poets and painters. Tatiana Zuniga and Alexis Triana, vice-president and president of Las Romerías, invited me to exhibit my work the following year and it became an annual pilgrimage. There are simply too many wonderful artists to name them all but el Flaco, Roly, Charlie, las Perlas del Son, Aceitunas Sin Huesos, Buena Fé, Postrova, Eduardo Frías, Diego Cano and so many others have shown me nothing but kindness. I also met local photographer Juan Miguel Cruz as we bounded up the stairs of a house looking for a good vantage point to shoot from. He is truly one of the world's honourable men. His cousin, José Rodríguez, was once Fidel Castro's personal photographer, and was instrumental in organising my first exhibition in Havana.

One Sunday in the capital I went to the Callejón de Hammel to see Afro-Cuban rumba in the flesh. Leonel Cespedes immediately took me under his wing. He is a big man with a big and generous heart. His mother is also a great cook.

Back in London I must thank my business partner Ken Climie for the rash decision to help develop my career and Sarah Campion for all of her hard work.

Also Aubrey Kurlansky and Miranda Snow for their sound advice and their work in the graphical design of the book, and Luke Peters for my reluctant portrait.

I would also like to thank Sergio Valdés Dorta, Export Director of Havana Club for his foreword and Elizabeth Fitzherbert, for her sleeve notes.

Finally, and most importantly, I would like to thank the Cuban people in general and the individuals who appear in this book in particular. The book is a celebration of their undaunted spirit, their unbounded ability to generate joy in any situation and their all-consuming love for life.